Paul Marlor Sweezy

And the History of American Marxism

By

MARSH MILLER

Table of Contents

Racial radicalism in North America had a major effect on the area during most of the twentieth century. In recent decades, the United States (and Canada) have climbed to the top of the global capitalist hierarchy, resulting in a culture of unparalleled prosperity and consumerism that is incomprehensible to a large portion of the world's population. During the first part of the twentieth century, the United States ascended to the top of the world's financial, military, and imperialist powers rankings. Because of the dominance of American international economic institutions, as well as their military foundations and alliances that spread throughout the world, the United States was able to dominate the global marketplace in the second half of the twentieth century, allowing the United States to maintain its "informal" imperial status. When it came to left-wing action, whether in the shape of uprisings or legislative discussions, the power of U.S. imperialism was an essential and pressing consideration. Contrary to the extraordinary accumulation of wealth and power, American capitalism is characterized by the persistent creation of large areas of structural poverty and unemployment for American workers, deep-seated racial divides, environmental destruction throughout all of human history in the pursuit of profit, and marginalization for societies outside of its borders in defense of foreign investments and US interests.

These changes have forced the radical left in North America to grapple with a diverse range of theoretical and political problems. In the first place, the fast rate of expansion that occurred during the Great Depression of the 1930s and the stagflation shocks of the 1970s aroused widespread concern about the mechanics of capital accumulation in the world economy. What variables led to accumulation, and which elements contributed to stagnation, were identified? As previously stated, it was already clear at the beginning of the twentieth century that trends towards the concentration and centralization of capital serve as the primary agents for the accumulation of large international monopolies, rather than the mythical powerless enterprises that operate in perfectly competitive markets, as had previously been assumed. What consequences did monopolization have on capitalist competition, and what ramifications did this have on the ruling class structure in the United States, are now being investigated. Third, as a consequence of the rising globalization of capital, the increasing interchange and integration of world capitalism circuits has occurred as a result of the increasing globalization of capital. But the economics and politics of imperialism have managed to establish a rigid hierarchy between the centers of capitalism and the peripheries that are dependent on these centers of capitalism.

As the twenty-first century dawned, what were the limitations and opportunities faced by left-wing governments trying to break free from the imperialist yoke and chart a new path toward democratic and equitable development? Fourth, as a consequence of the growth of capitalist production, financial capital of all sorts seemed to increase in unison with the rise of the productive potential of industrial capital. As a consequence, financial innovation, speculation, and the power of Wall Street increased throughout both times of prosperity and hardship. Whose ideas of capitalist development and financialization had the most impact on the Marxist theory of capitalism's growth and crises of financialization, and which theories were the most influential? The dominance of financial capital in the United States has resulted in a number of changes in the character of capitalism in the country. No matter how much market forces subordinated human labor to creative value and degraded employment in North America, radicals understood that there was no fundamental economic mechanism capable of producing an organically socialist and politically unified working class. What were the objectives for the cultural and organizational development of an independent working group that was beyond the authority of the two bourgeois parties that dominated American politics (as well as the social-democratic reformist party that ruled Canada)? When it comes to fighting for the communist cause, it is important to consider how an autonomous left might do so free of the suffocating legacy left by the Stalinist parties and their opponents.

It was the unique contribution of the American radical, Paul Sweezy, that allowed him to provide more innovative solutions to these urgent issues than anybody else in the world. Besides contributing to the creation of a place for formative Marxist thought in North America, he also sought to disseminate Marxist ideas across the rest of the globe.

Radical American

One would expect a descendant of the American ruling elite to have anticipated anything of this magnitude.

In his quest to become the next generation of leaders, Sweezy, the son of a Wall Street banker, passed through the hallowed halls of Exeter and Harvard, where America was grooming its future generation of leaders.

In his years as a student and collaborator at Harvard during the 1920s and 1930s, Sweezy met and collaborated with many of the country's finest thinkers, including Taussig, Hansen, Schumpeter, Lerner, Galbraith, Lange, Leontief, Samuelson, and many more. Sweezy was a student and collaborator of a wide range of economists, including Taussig, Hansen, Schumpeter, Lerner, Galbraith, Lange, Leontief, Samuelson, and others. His work was original from the beginning, yet it stayed within the confines of conventional economic theory throughout his career. The main focus of the book was on the economics of monopolies, and Sweezy made many contributions, including the now-standard neoclassical concept of a "sloping demand curve" as well as a single historical analysis of monopoly pricing in the coal sector.

He was on his way to Marxism and the inevitable upheaval that would accompany the Great Depression, and he didn't even realize it.

He made a major contribution to the subject when he wrote his contribution in 1942, The Theory of Capitalist Development, an outstanding article that was published in 1942.

At that time, the most current Marxist economic writing assessment, as well as an original evaluation, were both made available for viewing.

Capitalism is now experiencing a period of stagnation.

In the article, the Bortkiewitz solution, as well as other ideas, were discussed.

"Transformation issue" is used to differentiate between quantitative and qualitative problems when making a distinction between the two types.

Other problems include the question of qualitative value, the difference between Marxian and Ricardian economic theories, and others.

Setting a precedent for value-form assessments in the present day The Capitalist School of Thought is a school of thought that believes that capitalism is the best form of government.

Sweezy's goal of integrating Marxism into society and gaining recognition for it was marked by a dedication to the advancement of mankind.

Contribute to the development of a serious and genuine culture by becoming an active participant in our nation's intellectual life.

"The Marxism Brand in North America," says the author.

A term of duty in the Strategic Services Office followed by a period of service elsewhere

Sweezy was famously turned over for a position at Harvard because of his views on the war, despite the fact that Schumpeter was also passed over.

As samples of what you may anticipate, two books, a number of significant articles, and the co-founding of the review are all available on request.

In economics, economic studies are considered a subdivision of economics. As the American Academy of Marxism, the intellectual home of Marxism in the United States, opened its doors, this phrase greeted guests.

The narrowness of the offers at the top institutions in North America has remained, despite the fact that competition among them has increased. From that point on, everything changed.

Sweezy was a member of Henry Wallace's progressive party and the creator of the Monthly Review, which was published in London.

Leo Huberman is the publisher of "An Independent Socialist Magazine," which is well-known for its independence. He lives in New York City with his wife and two children.

The Monthly Review Press was established as a result of this event. There has been an excess of comparable accomplishments in recent history.

It was in the 1950s when McCarthyism, a kind of state-sponsored harassment and persecution, first appeared (with Sweezy)

The state of New Hampshire has brought a significant academic freedom case before the Supreme Court, which is now pending.

Sweezy, on the other hand, made significant contributions to American Marxism that did not end there.

On the basis of these considerations, it was determined to approach the evaluation of capitalism's development from two quite different perspectives. Sweezy had been a member of this group.

Contributions to the key 1950s discussion on the transition from feudalism to capitalism were important.

Hotels such as Hilton, Dobbs, and others are available. Sweezy's starting point was the overthrow of feudalism, which served as his inspiration.

Taken into consideration in the context of the global market environment and the function of profitable exchange in metropolitan areas,

A significant amount of effort was expended by centers in the formation of capitalist social production relations, in particular.

While Paul Baran released his classic book in 1966, Monopoly Capital published its classic book in 1966: an essay on the nature of money.

The New Monopoly, as he described it in his book American Economic and Social Order, was the most recent phase of capitalism's monopoly, which he labeled "the New Monopoly."

Following Baran's political economy of 1957 and the surplus approach,' there was a period of transition.

Michael Kalecki and Josef Steindl attempted, but failed, to establish a connection between monopoly pricing and economic development.

It was the goal of this study to comprehend not just the roots of the post-war boom, but also some of its limits in terms of dynamic performance.

avoid the entrenchment of stagnation and irrationality within the ruling elite, as well as social interactions supported.

The study of Monopoly Capital demonstrated Sweezy and Baran's deep unhappiness with the current order in the United States, as well as their understanding of the limits of overthrowing the present system.

It is rather their anti-capitalist policy successes that they put a high value on, as opposed to their economic achievements.

Zones emerged (reminiscent of today's anti-capitalist movements searching for a more equitable society), and they were divided into three categories:

It is becoming more common in North America to see peripheral alternatives to neoliberal centralization emerge.

The Monthly Review's open hostility to communism in the 1950s is a good starting point for understanding its current stance.

The Korean War is distinguished by the presence of a diverse variety of anti-colonialist organizations of various sorts. It also had a number of benefits as a consequence of the situation.

Defensive operations against revolutionary governments such as those in China, Chile, Vietnam, and other countries have been important. Cuba is the nation in its entirety.

In addition to being significant from a political perspective, these journals were an essential component of the global community.

However, Sweezy was also well-known for other topics outside his practical studies, which were published in the Monthly Review of Solidarity, which was founded by Sweezy.

Perspectives on the transition from socialism to capitalism are discussed in this article. It is possible to notice this later element in his work.

He and Charles Bettleheim had a well-known discussion regarding post-revolutionary civilizations, which is still remembered today.

Sweezy's investigation led to the discovery of the deepening of class divisions and the restoration of capitalism.

As a consequence of his activities, he said, the disciplining and separating elements of capitalism's global market had been reinforced.

In the absence of market processes, social divides between classes would deepen and reorganize, resulting in an increase in inequality.

capitalism. In order to combine socialist policy planning and defense mechanisms with other policies, it is essential to do so.

Decentralization initiatives are being made in order to encourage employees to take the initiative and embrace accountability.

The economic issues that plagued the world in the 1970s, as well as neoliberal development, have reappeared in the present day.

Sweezy's main focus is on the political economics of American capitalism, which he describes as "political economics of American capitalism." In the aftermath of the death of

In the 1960s, Harry Magdoff worked with Sweezy as co-editor of the Monthly Review, which was published by the University of Chicago Press. Leo Huberman is a well-known novelist who has written many books.

The bulk of his work is now created in cooperation with others (at the time of writing).

According to them, the upheaval of the 1970s was a watershed moment in history.

All indications were that the economy was heading back into stagnation, replete with all of the capacity limitations associated with Keynesianism.

Resolve the economic restructuring that has been evident in an age of monopoly capitalism for the second consecutive time.

That is, however, the end of the story.

The traditional deflationary stagnation is not the only problem: in recent years, stagnation has been linked to inflation and a depreciation of the currency, as well as other factors.

There is another financial explosion taking place. The ramifications of an excessive accumulation of relative production capacity

As a consequence, financial and money-capital outlets were now considered to be part of the economic outlet spectrum. That was the situation.

His last works, which were released in the 1990s, continue to deal with the same subjects.

Growing the quantity of financial capital accessible and making it more broadly available as a process typical of the financial sector.

Capitalism has been around from the beginning of time, according to historians.

Contributions come in at number two on the list of priorities.

Because of the broad breadth of his work, it is difficult to incorporate all of Sweezy's contributions to Marxian theory in one article.

In this course, you will learn about political economics as well as radical critiques of capitalism that are prevalent in North America today. However, it is not completely out of the question.

In order to bring attention to specific topics and significant comments made throughout a few of the discussions

In the United States, there is a strong focus on socialist principles.

Economic Stagnation with The Growth of Capitalist Society:

With a great Marxian evaluation at its core, capitalist development theory incorporates a number of additional aspects.

In the field of economics, a preliminary evaluation of capitalism's tendency to stagnate is given.

Sweethearts, there were twelve of them.

His study into the analytical gap between quantitative and qualitative values served as the beginning point for his whole investigation of the subject.

It is explained what the problems are, as well as an overview of Marxian crisis theory. In accordance with the preponderance of empirical economic theory

Sweezy was under the impression that he had rejected the decline in profit theory on the grounds that it was not supported by the data at the time.

It is inevitable that the biological composition of the capital would increase faster than the rate of surplus value, as a consequence of all of these causes. While Sweezy believes that capitalism's ills may be solved via socialism, others disagree.

> ...is found in the recognition that there is a conflict between production goals that are considered a natural-technical process for producing value and the recognition that there is a conflict between production goals that are considered a natural-technical process for producing value and the recognition that there is a conflict between production goals that are considered a natural-technical process for producing value and the recognition that there is a conflict between production goals that are considered a natural-technic process for producing value.

According to capitalism as a historical exchange-value development system, the following goals must be achieved:

It is a genuine phenomenon. It is not just an existential contradiction; it is the basic contradiction of everything.

The capitalism system is ultimately responsible for all of the contradictions that exist in the world.

Sweezy's thesis of underconsumption was presented in a rational and consistent way, and it has since gained widespread acceptance.

There is a line that can be traced back to Marx and Rosa Luxemburg in particular, and then to Michal Kalecki, and finally to the current day.

Joseph Steindl was a composer from Germany. However, due to the fact that it places a lesser focus on accumulation, it is more properly referred to as overaccumulation theory.

Because of a limited base of spending by workers, and, more significantly, because of an innate propensity to overspend

The rise in capacity for the production of consumer products will exceed the increase in consumer demand in the foreseeable future.

To put it another way, the ability of Department 1 to manufacture producer products is being assessed and quantified.

Department 2's desire for consumer goods is recognized as a fundamental problem, and it must be overcome.

The scope of capital reproduction has been expanded. Sweezy's guiding concept was one he never lost sight of, and it served him well throughout his life.

His first formulation of the issue was as follows: "Stagnation in production should be seen as natural when productive resources are being used below their maximum potential."

Capitalism's working conditions.... When this point of view is taken into account, the entire issue of the crisis is viewed in a new light.

The topic 'What causes crisis and depression?' is no longer the main center of debate. On the contrary, it says: 'What

Is it a source of expansion?'"

The rest of the book's ideas on monopolies were influenced by this.

State and market in every nation on the globe. Sweezy's investing problem, to paraphrase a sarcastic joke by Kalecki, is as follows:

It was beneficial in terms of increasing capacity.

While Sweezy's theorization enabled him to gain a deeper grasp of the patterns,

It also brought to light a number of issues linked to the reproduction required to keep capitalism development cycles continuing.

It is not entirely obvious why, for example, the market demand environment has stayed constant over the years.

Capitalism was created as a consequence of this. Examples include employees who produce the tools and equipment that are utilized in the manufacturing process.

Number of people who work rises when the industry's growth is sufficiently robust, thereby boosting demand

Consumable products are ones that can be eaten. Generally speaking, gross profit disbursements are a source of revenue.

As a consequence of excessive distribution and effective demand, while labor strains to achieve an increase in productivity

Another element is the added value, which includes things like interest payments, tax revenues, and so forth. This is the scenario.

Salaries are the most important element to examine because there is no theoretical reason why salaries cannot be raised.

In order to maintain accumulation while expanding output (or maybe by adding more value-added) (or maybe by adding more value-added),

Furthermore, it has been suggested that employees would have a propensity to establish collective bargaining agreements.

The present historical pattern is as follows: In any event, any inclination to command the social forces should be avoided.

The division of the value contributed has an impact on the specific reasons of class disputes and on the distribution of the value contributed.

They must be studied in terms of their historical background. A Thesis in Capitalist Theory stated by Sweezy

As a consequence, development was a specific Marxist argument - one that was employed against a number of other arguments.

Keynesians — most notably Alvin Hansen — have done a great job of balancing growth conditions.

In the framework of capitalist production relations, it appeared unlikely that demand would be fulfilled. But he was completely unaware of it.

Why should this be the case, and why does his list of underconsumption counter-forces — such as government subsidies.

New industries, trade, unsuccessful investments, and government spending all contribute to demand, but only to a limited degree.

Capacity, not the ability to succeed. His answer would be incorporated into his monopolistic competition theory of the market.

Monopoly Capital:

Sweezy did not put monopolization at the center of the development of capitalist stagnation in Capitalist Development Theory. Imperfect competition was only one of the factors that affirmed its effect on pricing power and earnings inclinations to stagnate. But in Monopoly Capital, Baran and Sweezy joined together in analyzing Josef Steindl's and Michal Kalecki's capitalist dynamics in order to explain why the stagnation is not a unique instance, but rather a generic case of monopoly capitalism. If capitalism rivalry inevitably drives the capitalist ability to generate value via the development of productive forces, the key issue is the mass of the surplus being generated and the circumstances under which it may be achieved. Baran and Sweezy argued that perfect competition among numerous capitals had now been dominated by imperfect competition between monopolies and that this fundamentally changed the conditions for achieving economic surplus. Indeed, a "law of increasing surplus" was created by monopoly capitalism, which extended the gross profit margin at certain operational levels.

This economic surplus may be computed at market prices in an original formulation as the whole actual (or potentially) production generated minus the socially required expenses, everything else such as advertising relies on the characteristics of the capitalist system. Most significantly, the fundamental issue of capitalist development vs stagnation is, with workers' wages relatively limited and capitalist profit margins increasing, as Kalecki long noticed, what the capitalists did with surplus. Baran and Sweezy claimed that the capitalist companies' spending outlets on consumption and out-of-profit investment tended to slow down their potential surplus. It follows that companies run under-use current capacity in a state of stagnation. Therefore, it is essential to combat demand-enhancing trends such as increasing sales, financial speculation and militarism. In other words, American capitalism's "hopelessly illogical system." Without this irrationality, "stagnation is a natural condition of the capitalistic monopoly economy.... left to itself ... the capitalism of monopoly would fall further and deeper into a swamp of chronic melancholy."

This conceptual shift to focus the notion of the 'economic surplus' on the 'excess value' has undoubtedly brought certain theoretical modifications.

Notably, the active social agency of employees in the creation and distribution of value-added issues is subjugated to systems-wide issues of excess absorption. This meant no small analytical expenses in terms of evaluating the capitalist dynamics and labor process and addressing American working class political development. However, it is not obvious enough that it meant abandoning the theory of work value that is so frequently unfairly accused that for some other analytical purposes it juxtaposes the realm of circulation with the sphere of production. Sweezy himself believed that his support (or that of Baran's) for the idea of labor value had not changed.

More significant, like Hilferding's Finance Capital Monopoly Capital has been quite unique in examining today's corporate organizational foundations, marketing and finance methods as well as its general system of governance. 7 Marxist study on the structure of contemporary companies and the consequences for capitalist dynamics and power remains much too little serious. But it is not clear why Baran and Sweezy's proposed market structure modifications should fundamentally change the impacts of competition on accumulation rather than tweak their shape. The strength of market pricing does not prevent the intensity of competition via technical development as companies strive to keep their share of the market space, new industries and developing and international competitive sectors. In this respect, as Lebowitz argued, monopoly capital is not a defect of pure capitalism, but a progression of the interior logic of capital to unification in order to boost the creation of value.

Sweezy himself gradually adopted this viewpoint, although he remained aware of the market structure of monopoly capital with an emphasis on the quantitative aspects of entry barriers, price power and differential profit rates. Notably, it was difficult to detect an increase in the pricing power of monopolies, decrease in workers' bargaining strength and a general shift in income distribution to capital before the economic crisis in the 1970s. While Sweezy's monopoly analysis of capitalism explained many of why debt growth and the types of responses from firms that took place through the 1980s would sustain stagnation, it blurred why international and domestic competition would escalate and become a core contradiction of neoliberal globalization and why American capitalism proved so robust and irritating

Financial Bang:

Capitalism in the 20th century was impossible to evaluate without considering financial capital in all its many forms and oscillations. Although, as Bellamy Foster pointed out, funding was never completely included in his theory of stagnation 19 Sweezy made a significant contribution to analyzing the 'financial explosion' that occurred in the context of the 1970s economic crisis. In his first work, Sweezy identified the interlocks in the composition of the U.S. ruling class between financial and industrial interests. Yet he criticized Hilferding in

The Theory of Capitalist Development for over-stressing financial capital "since the dominance of bank capital is a transitory phase of capitalist development." Industrial monopolies may use their differential profit rates more to depend on internal company financing instead of the banking system.

The 70s crisis meant that Sweezy once again saw the overwhelming propensity to stagnate in capitalist growth. With the failure of investment, the creation of systemic excess capacity, and a shift to salaries and government austerity, Sweezy (with his letter now most often written together with Magdoff) argued that the critical demand offset for economic crisis and stagnation was consumer, business and government debt. Instead of increasing production and employment, the consequences of monopoly competition were to reduce Keynesian fiscal and monetary incentives to inflation. In fact, while productive capital stagnated, money-capital was prosperous. The new financial innovations and growth of pure credit money helped to achieve this "financial boom," but its fundamental driver remained stagnation. Monopolies concentrate wealth and income more and more without making them viable avenues for genuine investment.

According to Sweezy and Magdoff, there was thus an increasing excess "into purely financial channels that gave birth to a growth of the financial superstructure of the economy and an unprecedented explosion of all sorts of speculative activity."

The debt mountains and deeper cycles of financial speculation have been unavoidable effects of mature capitalist monopoly. In fact, Sweezy came to the complete circle in his last writings on globalization: monopoly capital had developed into a "triumph of financial capital," now the main center of economic and political power.

Indeed, Sweezy's remarks were always sloppy on the problems presented by financial activity, with Magdoff's works trenching both social analysis and economic research. However, the circuitous thesis on the decline and rise of finance shows that money and output are not easily incorporated into the circuit of capital in its stagnation hypothesis. This is perhaps the place in which Keynesianism is implicitly penetrating Sweezy's conceptualization of financial activity in parallel as a purely speculative and rentier (although never falling into Keynesian subjectivism, money is merely a fiction and the object of accumulation rather than social rights). However, in addition to carrying speculative excesses at times, the function of financial capital in allocating money capital and providing credit to the most lucrative enterprises performs a vital role, without any other societal recourse than the pursuit of pure value for money.

And in this bank capital, as figuratively, the core nervous system of capital accumulation, has always had some institutional character in capitalism, separate from industry. And new financial innovations which extend bank capital's capacity to spread risk through hedge funds and other derivative markets are having the effect, on the one hand, of pre-validating credits and therefore the sum of future-calculating speculative funds, while, on the other, underwriting new companies and increasingly more and more complex fixed capital investments. If Sweezy's papers alert us to the speculative elements of finance, and especially to the rapid credit expansion as a new and fundamental characteristic of US capitalism, an integrated theory of financial capital must take on all of the forms credit-money affects capitalist economy.

Imperialism and Dependency:

Sweezy has always viewed the accumulation processes as developing productive forces and their interrelation with the sequence of exchanges forming the capitalist global market. This is his assessment of the market as one of the factors that contribute to the transition to capitalism, stimulated changes in social relations in the urban centers, and transformed suburbs through primitive accumulation. Imperialism as with Lenin is recognized as a distinguishing characteristic of the monopolized stage of capitalism in The Theory of Capitalist Development and a significant part of the book is dedicated to it. Here, imperialism stems from expanding the output of fixed capital as a natural process of capitalist growth compared to increasing demand for consumer goods. As the dominance of the propensity to overaccumulation compared to consumption grew with monopolization, imperialism intensified. In a paragraph today, Sweezy pointed out that ...the fresh rise of empires and militarism's resurgence entail an increase in the authority and scope of the state. The mature conflicts in the accumulation process in the nine eras of imperialism offer a further basis for increasing state action, especially in the economic sector.

Modern imperialism was a historic expression of monopoly capitalism, looking for ways to absorb the economic excess through exporting capital.

The topics which Sweezy had addressed with Baran's Political Economy of Growth were important to the effects of central accumulative dynamics on 'backward areas,' starting with the periphery's position in global capitalism.

This was discovered in the manner that primitive accumulation processes included non-western areas in the emerging global market. Colonial penetration started a historic process by which domestic class formations absorbed – or prevented from developing – the real economic surplus generated on the periphery, thus blocking the growth of capitalism along the same road as advanced capitalist zones. The worldwide division of labor, trade relations and the structuring of the economy for profit undoubtedly brought capitalism to life, but it was a skewed capitalist growth. Moreover, new financial-capital processes and monopolies proceeded to drain the economic surplus from the peripheries to the centers. Baran and Sweezy claimed in Monopoly Capital that 'save for the short time of unusually large capital exports to industrialized nations, foreign investment must be seen as a means of draining excess from undeveloped regions, rather than as a conduit to transfer surplus into them.'

These were all the fundamental elements of imperialism's understanding of 'dependence theory,' and Sweezy and Monthly Review were founders, putting special empirical attention to the role played by American imperialism in Latin America and Indochina.

As Sweezy phrased it, capitalism is "a global system which includes both (relatively few) industrialized nations and (relatively many) satellites and dependents."

Paradoxically, for the liberal idea of modernization, economic backwardness was not caused by a lack of capitalism but by capitalist modernization as a global market process. But Sweezy's general view has now also had a terrible ironic twist: the export of capital to absorb the created excess in the economic centers in turn has caused a surplus backflow, aggravating system-wide stagnant problems. The fundamental conflict in capitalism's economic structure has fallen between the developed and undeveloped regions, not within the center itself.

Like Magdoff's parallel imperialism, Sweezy's writing was one of the first to revisit the nature of the post-war world market, and he still reads remarkably fresh in comparison with the technological determinism of contemporary politics in globalization and considers the marginalization of the State and the US as an integral part of the world market. The weight of the explaining of the hierarchy of the global market, however, depends on trade connections and the political power behind them and how trading links have influenced domestic class structures. There were certain limits to how this properly penetrated the varied class configurations of states and the specific characteristics of the connections between exploitation, appropriation and work processes at various locations. For example, many emerging nations' relations of production were frequently very precapitalist, with little to do with widespread commodity exchanges and free labor, even as their surplus output was more available on the global market.

Exchange relationships typically strengthened, not weakened, pre-capitalist class relations. In other instances, capitalist social connections were clearly established and production forces started to build systematically, and this had to be examined thoroughly by themselves. Even if a national bourgeoisie was thoroughly infiltrated and corrupted, as with many of the Eastern Asian industrialized nations, some countries made considerable progress towards the levels of development of the economic centers. In even less tragic instances, however, capital systematically increased, causing significant change in class relations, although the relative income and inequalities in growth were not consistently closed to economic centers. In fact, the global market showed exceptional stability in the hierarchical connections between states, contrary to the neoliberal thesis of the equalizing world markets with zones established as capitalism.

Sweezy and dependence rightly insisted on this harsh truth. However, it proposed that the modalities of international exchange reinforced international hierarchies by free flow of commodities should be more carefully considered so that the value transferred from the peripheries to centers would allow for higher levels of investment, innovation and the development of productive forces. It also suggested that the class relations that were established in States as a result of internationalization and the interpenetration of capital were no longer essentially external: the internal integration of foreign capital within national governing blocs and domestic capitals was also peripheral to the international economic order. If so, the main line of the social divide could not be found on the world market between the centers and the peripheries, although it is still clearly a central feature of capitalism's uneven development, as Sweezy rightly pointed out, but it was within each state of the world market and its own particular class configurations and relations of production.

American Socialism

Sweezy's evaluation of the development of socialist politics in the United States under 'Third Worldism' has been given some easy judgment. This has to be stated more carefully. For Sweezy, revolutionary transformation was related to the formation of capitalism as a global system and the policy of absorption of the economic surplus. Given that both were driven by the processes of accumulation of capital, the integration of the workers into monopoly-capitalist and imperialist politics may be the fundamental strategic dimensions of socialist politics for Sweezy. In Theory of

Capitalist Development, he noted in the middle of the second World War that 'capitalist is still strong in the United States and the socialist forces are still insignificant.'

But socialism in many areas of the globe "may turn out in advance that imperialism has received a deadly blow from which it will never recover."

In this scenario, external outlets that compensate for stagnation would be shut off; sensible economic activity organization should be put on the agenda in order to compete with the competitor system. A peaceful transition to socialism was conceivable as an alliance of liberal reformers and socialists could go beyond the barriers of capitalist power to democracy. For a time of global upheaval and the People's Front, it made sense when systematic socialist progress appeared not only feasible but also probable. But Sweezy remained quiet on the growth of working-class politics in capitalist centers. Despair in the political environment in the centers gave way to optimism on the periphery.

Sweezy's political analysis recorded the growth of the Cold War and the absorption of U.S. unions and most of the left into the Democratic party. In both revolutionary and social-democratic parties, but taking part in the excess of the post-war period, American workers created a typical "labor aristocracy." Baran and Sweezy claimed in Monopoly Capital that working people had 'integrated' into the system in advanced capitalist nations and the hub of revolution had essentially moved towards the periphery zones. Industrial workers are, in the cited words of the book, a decreasing minority of the American working class, and their organized core elements in the fundamental industries have been widely incorporated into the system as customers and ideologically conditioned members.

They're not the particular victims of the system, as the industrial workers were in Marx's day... Of course, the system has particular victims. They are the jobless and the unemployed, the migrant agricultural laborers, the slum residents... the foreigners... If we focus just on the inner dynamics of advanced monopoly capitalism, it is difficult to escape the conclusion that if the possibility of effective revolutionary action is thin, the system may be overthrown.

But as they pointed out, the global market is capitalism, and the imperialist "exploited mass of these dependents" might be discovered as a revolutionary agency.

At the end of the day, the Baran and Sweezy evaluation was a hard but realistic interpretation of the balance of social forces in the US and of the battles at the time against American imperialism. It cannot be denied, moreover, that American radicals, above all others, must hold the US State accountable for U.S. imperialism and fully uphold the right of revolutionary regimes – and of reformists – to build alternative development routes from – and to modify – their relationship with world capitalism.

But which social actors are going to further the anti-imperialist fight in the US? Intellectual dissidents such as Sweezy himself, of course, and Monopoly Capital have drawn a line from there towards disadvantaged people of color in the U.S. To a certain degree plausible, but at the same time profoundly unsatisfactory responses in the sixties: the development of the essential socialist and working-class internationalism left to others other than the American working class.

This was obviously a mis calibrated approach for establishing sustainable socialist policies in the US that are needed to continue fighting against imperialism. The working-class agency has been grossly under-theorized. It implied that a single interest of the working class was consistently reformist once it had not become revolutionary in the course of capitalist growth and could only be disturbed by external actors. However, as Harry Braverman herself said in Labor and Monopoly Capital32, the interests of the working class are profoundly complicated and need to be challenged, not 'essentialized,' as one thing or the other. In a relative isolation from American workers, Baran and Sweezy's approach advocated the anti-imperialist policy and socialist strategy. This was a technique that was quite unique to the United States. In Canada, the New Left carried these similar battles into the union movement and created a real anti-imperialist, socialist current within the Canadian working class, which cannot even be generalized. 33

During the 1970's striking waves and the first battles against neo-liberalism, Sweezy permitted more tolerance to radical labor. But he didn't change his evaluation. At the end, as Marx's legacy reflected, he said that "the opinion that the proletariat in the advanced nations is destined to be an agent of revolutionary change is not realistic." 34 Silences persist on the political strategy for the formation and agency of the working class in the USA.

Political Deadlock

Sweezy brought up more new avenues of thought within Marxist theory than almost any other 20th-century Marxist economist in the area of the political economy as a whole.

Without his contributions, it is difficult to even conceive American Marxism. The stag-nationist theoretical viewpoint explained many things as to why structural crises tend to recur instead of creating a new boom immediately, and how monopolization creates new competitive situations instead of just quantitatively reducing them.

Stagnation remained in all Sweezy's works the normative conception of capitalism. This undercut idealized neoclassical market theorizations, indicated the limitations of Keynesian redistributive strategies and obliged Marxist theory to explore a variety of new issues. The resilience and dynamics of capitalist growth across the world and the reasons why American capitalism did not spiral into a spiral of decay and fad. It revealed far less.

This, it must be emphasized, is also the sense of the contribution of Sweezy to American radicalism.

No one else has done more to establish the independent socialist left's intellectual integrity. This is especially the position of Sweezy and Monthly Review. He realized early that the existing Communist parties – and its counterpart in the Trotskyist movement – had become more barriers for American socialism than paths ahead. Similarly, social democracy (including its Democratic Party component) has made peace with capitalism for a long time. This political clarity did not mean to push a sectional line against these parties, but instead, it supported the independence of radical new movements in their struggles – such as black liberation, feminism and environmentalism, and insisted that a new policy formation is an essential development for a viable socialist policy in the U.S. This was, of course, the distinguishing characteristic of North America's New Left. And socialist and Marxist thought was established as an essential part of the American and Canadian intellectual landscape. But here was also the stalemate of the politics of Sweezy and the New Left. Organizational experiments in creating a new socialist policy have been ephemeral, and are now a minor undertaking under the weight of neoliberalism. Criticism is in place of all the faults of American business and society and these flaws have never been more apparent to everyone. Sweezy did more to point them out than anyone else.

But seldom has the North American Left been less organized and idealistic, challenging our ability to transcend the limitations of capitalism. We know what we don't want to be, but we hesitate to imagine, express and fight for what we want to be. Paul Sweezy would have insisted on continuing the criticism of American capitalism with its fearless and moral necessity for reimagining and creating a new socialist project for North America, because of the barbarism that opened its doors in the 21st century with U.S. imperialism once again being a central agent.